The Cool Chameleon

Majo

ISBN: 1500955221
ISBN 13: 9781500955229

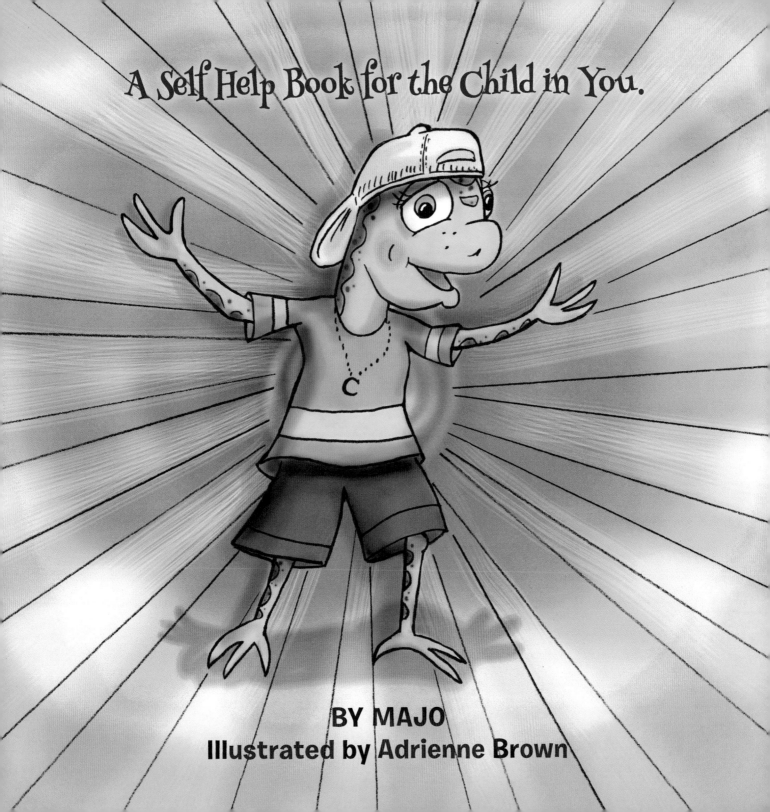

A Self Help Book for the Child in You.

BY MAJO
Illustrated by Adrienne Brown

Once there was a chameleon who thought he was very, very cool. A chameleon, as you may know, is a lizard-like animal who changes the color of his skin to adapt to any situation or environment he is in. Everyone liked this cool chameleon because he always became whatever they wanted him to be.

In the morning, he would wake up the damp grass by running through and teasing it with his song: "Oh, how I hate to get up in the morning!!!" The grass would laugh, but could never catch him because he could hide so well and mix right in.

Then, off he'd go to the flower beds. Soon his skin would turn a dark brown like the dirt that encased the flowers. As his skin changed, so did his mood... because flowers don't like to be teased or awakened abruptly. Flowers are delicate and easily hurt. The chameleon would adapt himself and become gentle with them. He made sure not to step on any petals because this might make them quite upset.

The chameleon would always act very cool around the flowers, but he did not stay too long. For, although he was adaptable and could fit right in, he felt uncomfortable. At times, he was not quite sure if the gentle flowers wanted him trampling through their beds.

Now, up the big palm tree the chameleon would start to climb. As he went, his dark brown skin changed to a khaki-colored tan. He wanted to complement the palm tree.

"Good morning, Mr. Palm Tree," he yelled. "Do you want me to scratch your bark today?"

"Yes, Chameleon, I would like that very much. I didn't sleep a wink last night. Mr. Blustery Wind had me up ... swaying back and forth and back and forth. Just when I thought I could catch some shut eye, he'd blow really, really hard. Oh boy, was that annoying!!"

The chameleon liked to help the palm trees. Mr. Palm Tree was so strong and handsome, while he himself was small and rather on the homely side. Hanging out with the big palm trees made him feel important. When he would cling to their trunks, it was as if he were one of them.

But he wasn't. Sooner or later, he would have to climb down and begin changing his color once again.

At the end of the day, the cool chameleon would wander to the beach and, for a brief time, walk unnoticed among the white sand.

"Gosh, I wish I could be different," he mumbled. "I wish I didn't have to change myself so much. It gets very tiring changing my color all the time. Sometimes, I don't know if I'm the right color or not. Why, just last week I didn't turn green quickly enough and the grass got super mad at me. They thought I was trying to stand out and be different. They called me a show off.

You know, at times it all seems very confusing. I'm not sure who I really am."

"Who are you talking to?"

"Who's that?"

"It's me, Mr. Crab."

"You weren't supposed to be listening," said the startled chameleon. "Don't you know it's impolite to eavesdrop?"

"I wasn't eavesdropping." said Mr. Crab. "You were talking out loud. How could I not hear you? And by the way, it sounds like you could use some help."

"You're just an old crab," said Chameleon. "What could you possibly know about someone as complex as me? You never change. You just stay the same. You're not as lucky as I am. I can change and become any color I want.

I can be blue as the sky, green as the ocean, or white as the sand. But you!! You're even uglier than I am, with no hope of ever changing."

"But I like being a crab, and I don't think I'm ugly at all."

"Ha, ha, ha," laughed Chameleon. "Have you seen your reflection in the water lately?"

"I don't have to", smiled the crab. "I know what I am. I'm happy being a crab. I don't have to change myself. I don't have to twist myself up like a conch shell in order to be cool. So what if I can't change the color of my shell. I have big eyes, strong claws, and I'm an excellent swimmer."

"Yeah, and you're also conceited. Beat it crab," snarled Cool Chameleon, feeling rather annoyed.

"Boy, are you a grouch!!!"

"Oh no I'm not", answered the chameleon. "No one likes grouches. But everyone likes me because I'm so cool and adaptable."

"Everyone's grouchy sometimes," Mr. Crab mused. "We all get a little scared now and then. There are even days when we're not quite sure who we are... or if others like us or not. I know I have days when all I want to do is bury myself in the sand and hope nobody finds me."

Cool Chameleon looked at the crab quizzically. "I thought I was the only one who sometimes feels afraid, who sometimes worries whether others liked me or not. Many times I want to stay hidden, so that no one will bother me. Some days I even wish I were someone else. Do you ever think like that?"

"Well, I used to," said Mr. Crab. "But I don't anymore. I would look up at the sky, wish I could fly like the pelicans and dive for my food... instead of having to crawl on all tens. Then, for a while, I wished I were a barracuda, one of those mean looking fish that scare the shell right off ya. I thought if I were one of them I'd have nothing to fear. I wasted so much time wishing I were someone else.

But alas, I'm a crab and that's not so bad. Actually, it's pretty good. You know, Chameleon, it's all about how you look at yourself."

"What made you change?" the chameleon asked.

"I wasn't happy," answered Mr. Crab. "I kept trying to be something I wasn't."

"I know what you mean," Chameleon whispered. "I want to be just plain me. But when I'm around others, I think I have to change to be what they want me to be."

"Have you ever tried just being yourself?" asked Mr. Crab.

"I've thought about it lots of times," said the chameleon. "But I'm afraid others won't like me if I'm not what they want."

"Ah ha!!!" shouted the crab. "Cool Chameleon always trying to make others happy. Don't you see? In the end, you're the one who's not happy. Did you ever think they might like you more if you were just yourself?"

"But... suppose they don't? Suppose they wind up not liking me at all. Suppose they don't let me play with them anymore? What will I do then?" the chameleon cried.

Mr. Crab consoled the chameleon. "There are no easy answers. But when you are true to yourself, you will feel happy and carefree... kind of like a balloon floating in the big, beautiful, sunlit sky."

"You're kidding me, right," smiled Cool Chameleon.

"Don't get me wrong," replied the wise crab. "There may be times when you will be scared and want to go back to your old ways. But, trust me, you won't like how you will feel."

"How will I feel?" asked Chameleon.

Mr. Crab looked at the chameleon thoughtfully. "Even though you will be surrounded by others, you will feel sad and lonely."

The chameleon shivered..."Oh boy. That's not good."

"No, it's not. Stop pretending to be something you're not. Just be yourself!" declared Mr. Crab. "If you do, you will walk tall in the green grass. You'll stand proud among the pretty flowers. You'll feel as big and strong as the mighty palm trees."

"It sounds too good to be true," sighed the chameleon.

"Sure, I thought so too," laughed the wise old crab. "But until you try it, you will never know for yourself."

"I don't know if I am strong enough to just be myself," Chameleon replied weakly.

"I can help you," offered Mr. Crab. "I cannot go with you for my home is in the sea. But you can come to me when you're sad or lonely... or if you just need someone to talk to. I'll be glad to listen.

Chameleon, we all need someone we can turn to. We all need someone who likes us just the way we are."

"But chameleons aren't supposed to hang out with crabs. It isn't cool."

"Says who," snapped Mr. Crab.

"I don't know. It's just the way it is", Chameleon replied sheepishly.

"There you go again, doing what you think others want you to do. And you don't even know why! Don't you ever think for yourself?" shouted Mr. Crab. "That is definitely not cool...NOT cool at all."

The crab looked at the chameleon...waiting for an answer.

"Well... yeah... eh... sure I do... maybe. Oh, I don't know. All I know is I like to make others feel happy and comfortable." Chameleon stammered.

"And what about you, Chameleon. Are you happy? Are you comfortable?"

Cool Chameleon didn't answer the crab. He just stared out at the clear blue water.

"Come on, Chameleon," encouraged Mr. Crab. "What do you say... What do you have to lose... Just be yourself... Be the best you... Why don't you give it a try........"

AUTHOR BIOGRAPHY

Majo is a wife, mother, grandmother, writer and entrepreneur who promotes positive thinking, and achieving a high quality of life. While raising her family, she began her career as a corporate consultant, training employees in team building, sales and diversity. She also earned a real estate license, wrote a column called "The Family Hour" for a Philadelphia area newspaper and modeled in print and television. She founded three businesses to foster personal accountability, successful parenting and improving the prevalent cultural mindset regarding women in advertising.

Of all her many accomplishments, Majo is most proud of being the mother of her eight children and the grandmother of many. Majo is a beautiful, energetic and determined entrepreneur. *"The Cool Chameleon"* is the second book in a six book series. It has taken her 30 years and many, many rejection letters to achieve this goal. The saying "It's never too late" and Bob Dylan's quote "He who is not busy being born, is busy dying" motivate Majo to keep growing.

Majo is married and lives in Smithville, NJ.

Contact Majo at her website:
majo the author.com or email her at mjbgd@aol.com

Made in the USA
Charleston, SC
14 August 2015